WICKET-KEEPING

WICKET-KEEPING

BY
MAJOR R. T. STANYFORTH,
THE ARMY, YORKSHIRE AND ENGLAND.

The Naval & Military Press Ltd

Published by

The Naval & Military Press Ltd
Unit 5 Riverside, Brambleside
Bellbrook Industrial Estate
Uckfield, East Sussex
TN22 1QQ England

Tel: +44 (0)1825 749494

www.naval-military-press.com
www.nmarchive.com

In reprinting in facsimile from the original, any imperfections are inevitably reproduced and the quality may fall short of modern type and cartographic standards.

PREFACE

I AM tempted to write this book, as for many years I have searched for a book on wicket-keeping from which I could gain some information, or, at any rate, food for thought. There does not seem to be such a thing. In most books on cricket the subject is dismissed in a page or two of generalities, in platitudes such as " a wicket-keeper must be able to stand hard knocks!" I was horrified to see an International cricketer state in an authoritative book on cricket " that if a professional wicket-keeper was not available, the school coach could, at any rate, offer a few hints such as *the necessity of keeping both feet absolutely still and pivoting from side to side from the hips alone!*"

I have endeavoured in the following pages to point out the principles and also the varied aspects of wicket-keeping, together with some hints as to how the many difficulties can be overcome.

I should like to think that they may be of practical use to young wicket-keepers, and that they may give non-wicket-keepers a rather closer insight into a most important and interesting department of the game of cricket.

The late William Storer, who kept wicket for Derbyshire and England, and was in his prime in the nineties, taught me such wicket-keeping as I know, and even if he did not make a very good job of it I am ever grateful to him for the many happy days I have spent keeping wicket in England, South America, South Africa, the West Indies and Egypt.

R. T. S.

ENGLAND *v.* AUSTRALIA, 1934.
Oldfield 'keeping to O'Reilly ; Wyatt (and Hendren) batting.
An example of perfect wicket-keeping.

CONTENTS

CHAP.		PAGE
I.	QUALIFICATIONS	1
II.	TAKING THE BALL: GENERAL PRINCIPLES	5
III.	TAKING THE BALL—*Continued*	10
IV.	CATCHING	17
V.	STUMPING	20
VI.	RUNNING OUT	23
VII.	BYES	26
VIII.	APPEALING	28
IX.	CARE AND REMEDIES FOR THE HANDS ...	30
X.	EQUIPMENT	34
XI.	WICKET-KEEPING AND BATTING	38
XII.	BOWLERS AND WICKETS	41
XIII.	MAKING A YOUNG WICKET-KEEPER	45
XIV.	PERSONAL REMINISCENCES	48
XV.	TEST MATCH WICKET-KEEPERS	52
XVI.	WICKET-KEEPING FEATS	55

CHAPTER I.

QUALIFICATIONS.

It is a hackneyed remark, and one that has not yet been either proved or refuted, to say that wicket-keepers are born and not made.

There appears to be no reason why any boy, or grown man for that matter, who has the natural attributes that go towards making a good fieldsman, should not make himself into a good wicket-keeper. The word fieldsman is used advisedly, as it is a curious thing that there are many absolutely first-class batsmen and bowlers who never have been, and never will be, anything but absolutely paralytic in the field. The late C. H. Titchmarsh was an outstanding case of a batsman, and there is a well-known amateur playing to-day who is a similar case of a bowler.

Anyone who wishes to become a wicket-keeper need not necessarily have the agility of a good fieldsman, but he must have the natural ability to catch a ball. This may possibly be innate, as it is interesting to watch a lot of children playing ball together. Some catch it quite instinctively; others have no idea at all, and seldom even get a touch.

There are two necessary qualities which are not essential in either the good fieldsman or the good average player of most games. There are:—(1) nerve; (2) an outstanding power of concentration. Whether these qualities are born or made it is difficult to say. The first is probably born in everyone, and subsequently preserved or lost; the second is probably latent at birth, and either cultivated or allowed to lie dormant later in life.

Nerve is dependent on general good health and general soundness. No one can expect to keep wicket when in indifferent health from any cause —in this aspect it should be noted that no one can keep wicket well if he has gone to bed too late the night before a match. He is sure to be just a bit below par, and his nerve will be affected. Nothing else but his nerve. The eye will probably, but not certainly, be all right. Batsmen constantly play the most beautiful innings after a very late night, or when they are really quite ill. G. E. V. Crutchley made 99 not out in a 'Varsity match with measles. Paynter came straight out of a sick bed in Australia to play a great innings in a Test Match. There are numerous such instances, but a wicket-keeper never gives of his best in such circumstances. Hospitably entertained touring teams should, at any rate, try to get their wicket-keeper to bed early.

A sore hand or finger which gives pain every time the ball is taken naturally makes good results impossible, but often an injury such as a slightly damaged thumb, or a sore shin bone, which may only be struck again once an hour, or possibly not at all, has a similar effect, because it reacts on the wicket-keeper's nerve. Similarly, a blow in the face in the previous match is very apt to produce a temporary loss of nerve.

But the most important point in this question of nerve, especially for young wicket-keepers, is never to keep on a bad wicket if it can possibly be avoided. Let schoolmasters and cricket coaches bear this continually in mind.

Even if the wicket-keeper does not get actually injured, and does not appear to mind the blows on wrists, shoulders, chest, and possibly face, which are inevitable on a bad wicket (it is amazing what some people can stand), it must very soon shatter his nerve, and he is soon drawing back a little with one foot, putting *his head in the air*, and being afraid to put his head across on the leg side out of the shelter of the batsman's body. The braver the wicket-keeper the less obvious becomes the reason for his lack of improvement and subsequent deterioration, but there it is.

Concentration.—A wicket-keeper's job is a whole-time one from the moment the first ball is delivered until he has either taken the last ball or it has been thrown in by the fieldsman.

From the time the bowler starts his run he must concentrate on thinking how and where he is going to take that ball. For this purpose he must first of all watch the bowler's hand very carefully to see what he is trying to do with the ball. He must, at the same time, be expecting the worst—such as a wide yorker on the leg. He must be prepared for all eventualities. It is not a bad plan for him to try and convince himself that he is going to be offered a chance off every ball. Never let him imagine that there is any likelihood of his not being required to take the ball. After a batsman has played the ball he must watch the fieldsmen until the ball is back again in the bowler's hand, waiting for the ball to be returned to him, or even in some cases backing up a return to the bowler. If once a wicket-keeper allows his attention to wander it is almost a certainty that a chance will be offered and not accepted.

Circumstances such as the following are conducive to a lack of concentration. The game has been going on some time—two batsmen are well set on a good wicket, playing nearly everything in the middle of the bat, now and again leaving a wide ball alone. Bending down and up, up and down, taking the wide ball occasionally, becomes mechanical, concentration is relaxed—click, and a catch is missed. "Whoever would have thought that this batsman, playing as well as he has been, would fail to cut a slow long hop like that!"

Another dangerous time—the end of a long day in the field. The wicket-keeper has kept very well. "Anyhow, there is three-quarters of an hour to go and only one wicket to fall. This batsman cannot last more than a few overs, and I shall catch the 6.5 train instead of the 7.10. I suppose that was a chance of stumping. Never mind, we shall get him out next over." But he plays out time till 6.30.

It is commonly said that the ideal position in the field for a captain is that of wicket-keeper. That may be, but the ideal position for a wicket-keeper is not that of captain.

You can point to a few instances of successful wicket-keeper captains. The latest example is that of Cameron, who kept wicket for and captained South Africa in their last team in Australia. But his wicket-keeping, it is said, lost a little of its former brilliance, and if this was so it was due, without doubt, to the cares of captaincy on the field.

It is nearly impossible for one person to combine the concentration necessary for the best of wicket-keeping with the continued thought that is required of a modern captain.

Captaincy of a side in the field becomes more scientific every day, and a modern captain should be thinking whenever he is not actually fielding a ball himself. He has a great many things to consider—the score, the time, the batsman's characteristics, the state of the wicket, his bowlers, the placing of their field, the saving of his bowlers' running and throwing—the last in itself gives him quite enough to think about. Modern freak fields and very often the necessity of " hiding " one or two fieldsmen make it all the more difficult. Especially at the beginning of an innings is this likely to occupy his mind, and it is at the beginning of the innings, when the ball is swinging, that chances are most apt to be given to the wicket-keeper. Number one batsmen, too, are rather apt to take advantage of an early let-off.

There is practically never a moment when a wicket-keeper is not fielding a ball or ready to do so, and it is too much to ask one man to combine the concentration and thought which are necessary for wicket-keeper and captain respectively.

Photo: Sport & General.]

PLATE I. ENGLAND *v.* AUSTRALIA, 1926.
Strudwick 'keeping behind Bardsley.

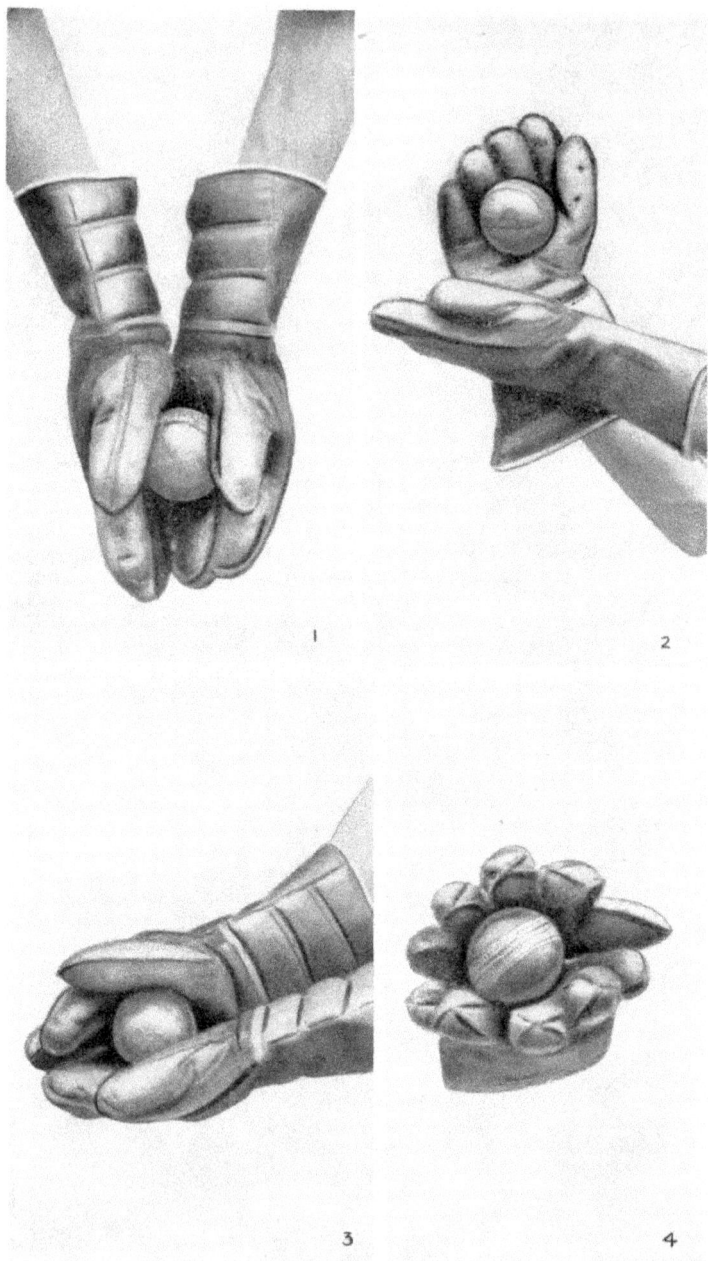

PLATE 2.

CHAPTER II.

TAKING THE BALL—GENERAL PRINCIPLES.

Hands.—There are two cardinal principles in taking the ball behind the wicket. The first is, never snatch—which, put it briefly, means that the hands must give a certain amount at the moment of impact with the ball. The amount depends entirely upon the pace of the ball, and in the case of a very slow bowler it becomes almost imperceptible, but it is there or should be, nevertheless. In point of fact more snatching is seen at slow bowlers than at fast, because the natural inclination is to allow the hands to give when taking a fast ball in order to minimize the concussion.

The other principle is to take every ball, wherever possible, with the fingers of both hands pointing to the ground. (See plate 1.) If this is done it makes it much more difficult to snatch, and the wrists are in such a position that they give a little naturally to the force of impact. The hands in this position form a natural cup, the centre of which is a point just below where the fingers join the palms, or what is really the opposite face of the knuckle joints. Here the ball should strike, and the four fingers of each hand grip it half involuntarily owing to the position of the hands, and half deliberately at the moment of impact. The thumbs close over it, and prevent it escaping on either flank. [See plate 2 (i).]

There comes a point, however, when the ball rises so high that it is obviously impossible to take it with the fingers of both hands downwards. It can be done to the waist or possibly a little above, but once the ball rises any higher the following method must be adopted. The ball must be taken, on the off side, in the right hand, the fingers of which should be extended straight upwards; the left hand is placed horizontally to the right, forming a cup just below it, with the fingers nearly at right-angles to the right wrist. The ball strikes the middle of the right hand, and the left hand then closes upwards and over it. [See plate 2 (ii).]

One of the reasons why rising balls are rather apt to be missed is that the little finger now has to form the outer flank guard, and is not so well fashioned to do so as the thumb. The same process is reversed when taking a rising ball on the leg side—the left hand being upright, and the right forming the horizontal cup.

This is an awkward and unnatural movement for a right-handed wicket-keeper, and should be practised, because it is one of the reasons why left-handed batsmen are rather a bugbear to the wicket-keeper who is not quite top class. It is an important ball to take, too, because most bowlers try to get a left-hander out with a rising ball on his off, taking advantage of that well known, but quite inexplicable, weakness of most left-handers. It is difficult to understand why they are so liable to cut at a wide, rising ball on their off side, but they undoubtedly are.

These, then, are the only two positions of the hands when receiving the ball behind the wicket, with the possible exception of the very wide ball which is taken by a compromise between the two positions. At full stretch of the arms the wrists cannot drop and the ball is taken in the right hand with the fingers pointing outwards, and the left hand forming a cup underneath it with the fingers horizontal or vice versa. [See plate 2 (iii).]

The one thing that must never be done under any circumstances is to take the ball in rat-trap fashion—that is, with the fingers of either hand pointing towards the line of flight of the ball. [See plate 2 (iv).]

It is obvious that, sooner or later (generally sooner) the ball will be received on the end of one of the ten fingers.

Even if it does get safely into the palms of the hands the wrists are not in a position to give to the force of impact, and the yielding has to be done by pulling the arms back.

A ball of normal height on the off side should, if possible, be taken more in the left hand than the right, and on the leg side more in the right hand than the left. There is a two-fold purpose in this. It allows a margin for the deflection of the ball at the last minute by the bat, and gives the ball a better chance of finishing up in the middle of the outside hand instead of on the thumb.

Also, if a wicket-keeper is forced away from the wicket and is off his balance a bit, with too much weight on the outside foot, he has the ball in the hand nearest to the wicket, and it is much easier and quicker to remove the bails with one hand than to sweep both hands to the wicket. (See plate 3.)

Photo: *Sport & General.*]

PLATE 3. ENGLAND *v.* SOUTH AFRICA, 1929.
Duckworth 'keeping behind Mitchell.

PLATE 4. GENTLEMEN v. PLAYERS, 1931.
Ames 'keeping to Verity. Duleepsinhji (and Jardine) batting.

[Photo: *Sport & General.*]

In the case of wide "throws in" when the wicket-keeper finds himself out of reach of the wicket, it often makes the whole difference in getting the bails off in time.

This method of taking the ball is of tremendous value. It obviously cannot always be done, but it is an ideal to aim at and to practise.

Feet.—There is much more footwork in wicket-keeping than most people imagine. Balance depends upon the position of the feet, and no one can go on taking ball after ball accurately in the hands without being properly balanced.

The first object is to start with the feet in a suitable position, and this is known as stance. In adopting his stance a wicket-keeper has first of all to consider where he can get the best view—unimpeded by the batsman—of the delivery of the ball. This is obviously either over or outside the off stump. But he naturally does not want to go farther than is necessary to the off, or it will make it increasingly difficult to get across to take balls outside the batsman's body on the leg side. The modern habit of crouching right down so that the tips of the fingers are touching the ground makes it imperative to have the head and body clear of the off stump. This means that the left foot is placed behind the middle stump or, possibly, middle and off, and the right foot is well clear of the off stump at a distance of about 18 inches from the left (measuring from toe to toe—the heels, of course, are closer together). The right foot must be the same distance from the crease as the left. It is a very bad fault to have it drawn back behind. The alternative and more old-fashioned method is to have the left foot on the middle and leg, which brings the right foot only just clear of the off stump, and only to bend down sufficiently to look *over* the top of the off stump.

The former is, however, the generally accepted stance of modern cricket. Probably its chief advantage is that it must bring the weight equally distributed on to the ball of the feet, and not the heels, this assuring a good balance and the ability to assume the next position in the minimum of time and with the minimum of effort. Plate 4 gives a good example of this stance.

The distance the feet should be behind the wicket and crease is easy to estimate. They must obviously be close enough to enable the hands to reach the wicket with ease and without stretching. On the other hand, they must not be so close that the bails are liable to be removed involuntarily either by the hands or by the top of the pad when bending down or moving the legs.

The next question which arises is how far are the feet going to be moved in order to assist the hands in receiving the ball.

The great thing to remember is that under no circumstances are the feet and legs to be moved for the deliberate purpose of stopping the ball unaided by the hands. It is a natural temptation which has to be resisted at all costs by young wicket-keepers. The legs do, as a matter of fact, naturally constitute themselves as a second line of defence, but they should never be relied upon, or regarded as such. The one object of a wicket-keeper is to get the ball in his hands.

Now, remembering that the object is to take the ball whenever possible with the fingers pointing to the ground, a practical experiment will show that this is impossible if the hands and arms are extended some distance beyond the body or outside leg. Keep the feet still and extend the hands as if to take a ball wide of the body. The wider the ball is the more horizontal become the fingers. Try moving the outside foot to bring it more or less in the line of flight of the ball, and the fingers naturally adopt the perpendicular position.

That, then, may be taken as a general and very simple guide, *i.e.*, that, on the off the right foot and, on the leg, the left foot should be carried off to a position on or just about the line of flight of the ball, in order to bring the hands into the proper position and, if possible, to take it with the inside hand.

Remember, though, that care must be taken to move the foot sideways only, and not backwards as well. This is a bad fault as it brings the body sideways, and with it the hands which no longer present the full face of the palms to the ball.

At the same time the foot must not go forwards, for that would bring it too near the crease and might result in the ball being taken in front of the wicket, or in avoiding this, the hands may find themselves pinned against the pads with no room to " give." Incidentally, this may happen sometimes even if the feet are in the right position, and it is often the cause of the lowish ball not being taken cleanly.

So much for the outside foot. Now what happens to the inside foot? A question which often puzzles young wicket-keepers, but which, in fact, answers itself. The inside foot—that nearest the wicket—quite naturally moves, more or less (generally rather less), a similar distance in order to take its share of the weight and maintain a perfect balance.

It should be a little shy however of following its colleague too far to one side of the wicket, as it has got to take the weight for a stumping movement, and is a guide to the wicket for the hands once they have received the ball. When the ball is in the hands and it is necessary to transfer hands and ball to the wicket, the inside leg must take the greater weight. (See plate 8.)

When the hands are receiving the ball the weight should be equally distributed on the whole of both feet, not only, of course, on the balls of the feet as in the original stance.

Unnecessary movement of the feet must be avoided. Some wicket-keepers jump about like a cat on hot bricks. A great proportion of balls bowled are directed on or about the off stump, and can be taken without moving the feet from their original position.

CHAPTER III.

TAKING THE BALL—*Continued*.

Off Side.—With regard to taking the ball on the off side there is little to add to what has been said in the last chapter of general principles.

Assuming that the wicket-keeper has watched the ball in the bowler's hand from the start of his run, has noted the spin or cut which has been applied to the ball, and has watched the flight, the last and most important indication he gets of the ultimate destination of the ball is to see it the moment it pitches. This is comparatively simple on the off side as the bat is the only thing which is going to obscure his vision, and the only occasion when the bat masks the pitch of the ball is in the case of over-pitched balls. In these cases it nearly always appears that the ball must hit the bat, and it generally does—but not always. A wicket-keeper must never allow himself to think that a ball must hit the bat. It is the cause of innumerable missed chances and byes.

Over the top or very adjacent to the wicket.—Balls which pass over the top of the stumps, or very adjacent to the off or leg stump, deserve a special short paragraph. They are the most difficult to take for the reason that the batsman's legs, body and bat are all in the wicket-keeper's line of vision. The pitch of the ball is often partially obscured, and he has to guess where the ball is going to appear and pick up its line of flight with great celerity after it has passed the obstructions. This really can only be done with constant match practice, and it is a sign of a high-class wicket-keeper to see the ball being taken cleanly over the top of the stumps, or an inch away, especially on the leg side.

There is again a fault which is committed by the best wicket-keepers of imagining that the ball must hit the wicket if it misses the bat. How often the batsman misses a ball which appears to be dead on the wicket. The wicket-keeper's hands go up, the ball just misses and four byes result. The newspaper comment reads that so-and-so, in his next over, defeated both batsman and wicket-

PLATE 5. GENTLEMEN v. PLAYERS, 1929.
Duckworth 'keeping behind Haig.

Photo: Sport & General.]

keeper. The wicket-keeper has been defeated partly because his vision of the ball has been obscured till the last possible moment, but he knows, or should know, more or less where that ball is going if missed, and his defeat is often due to the unwarrantable assumption that it must hit the wicket, and he has prematurely thrown up his head. Duckworth does not do so. (See plate 5.) A very large proportion of byes and sometimes missed catches are due to this assumption, that the ball must hit the wicket if it misses the bat.

Balls on the leg side.—These are the bugbear of the young or moderate wicket-keeper. Why are they such a bugbear? It is perfectly easy to take balls on the left of the wicket if there is no batsman, with the possible exception of the rising ball which was dealt with in the previous chapter.

It is obviously because there is a moment when the batsman's body completely obscures the view of the ball.

When it is considered what a short time even a slow ball takes from the moment it leaves the bowler's hand until it arrives at the wicket, it is not surprising that an interruption of that brief moment in which to follow the flight of the ball makes it very difficult, and the accurate taking of balls outside the batsman's body demands an exceptional quickness of eye and limb.

It also calls for more nerve, as naturally an interrupted view of the ball may result in the ball hitting some portion of the wicket-keeper before he gets his hands to it, and, furthermore, the bat is often brandished perilously near his head. See frontispiece.

In order to take leg balls cleanly it is absolutely essential to get a second sight of the ball after the interruption caused by the batsman's body, and it is quite useless to extend the hands vaguely in the hope of the ball finding its proper resting place, because it never does.

Wicket-keepers in village matches keep the byes down quite well by jumping with both legs together and making no attempt to use their hands. This is not wicket-keeping, but it is a makeshift due partly to the inability of the wicket-keeper, and partly to the inferiority of the wicket which really makes it impossible to do otherwise.

It is very regrettable though to see schoolboys being allowed to do it on a perfectly good wicket, while the cricket master, probably quite a good player himself, looks on.

In order to get this second view of the ball a wicket-keeper must have a very good idea of its line of flight after it has hit the ground. Therefore, the first essential is to see the ball pitch, if possible, before it is obscured by the batsman's body.

Plate 6 will show that the shorter the ball is the better view there is of its pitch, and the longer time there is, subsequently, to move across and pick it up again. The further up the ball is pitched the more difficult it is to see, as the line of sight passes through the batsman's arms and bat and, finally, there comes a point when the pitch of the ball cannot be seen before moving to the leg side of the wicket.

Experience will show that anything short of a half-volley, unless it is pretty wide, should be seen pitched from the off side before moving across.

Assuming, then, that the half-volley and everything else further up cannot be seen pitched from the wicket-keeper's original position on the off side of the wicket, it should be clear that, in order to take these balls, the wicket-keeper must move over before they strike the ground and, if possible, view the pitch of the ball from a position just outside the batsman's legs. This is not so easy, but it does give him a certain time to get over it, and after hitting the ground the ball has less time to rise or deviate from its original course before it reaches him. Over-pitched balls of this nature will invariably come below knee height as they have not yet reached the maximum of their rise off the pitch, unless by ill chance they strike turf which has been torn up by the bowler. This cannot be catered for. Mercifully, they seem more apt to shoot on these occasions, and it is only a question of four byes unless it hits the second line of defence, which it should do, rather than a bang in the chest or face.

The diagram should give some idea of what balls can and cannot be seen to pitch from the off side of the wicket, and of the wicket-keeper's vision as he moves across to the leg side, either to pick up the line of flight again after viewing the pitch, or to view pitch and line of flight simultaneously.

The footwork in taking a ball on the leg side is the same as that on the off side, the only difference being that there is a little further to go, as the wicket-keeper is standing more on the off side than on the leg in order, as we have seen, to get an uninterrupted sight of the delivery of the ball.

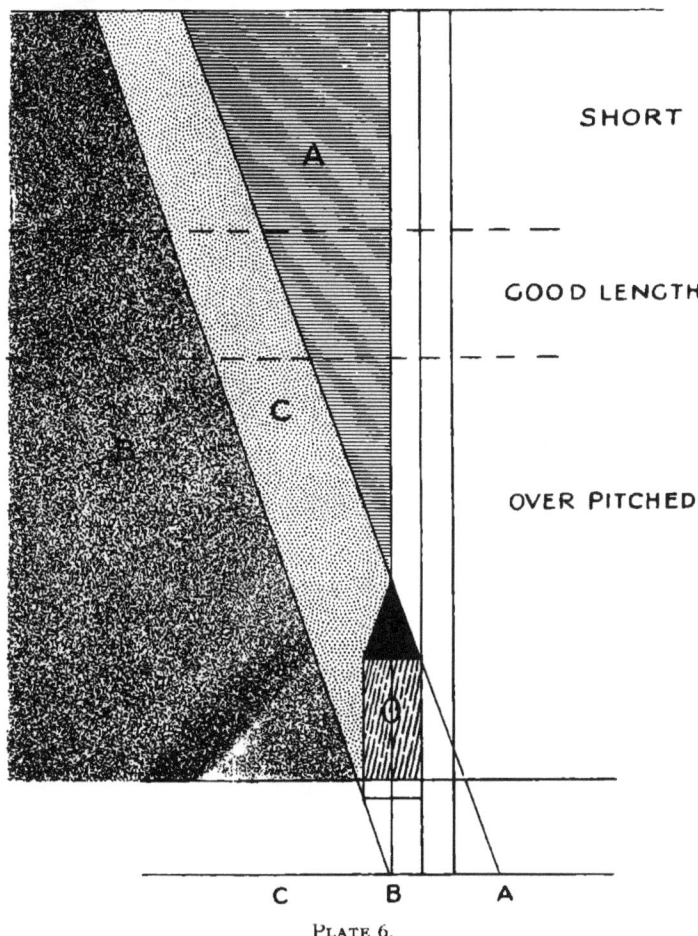

PLATE 6.

O is the obstruction caused by the batsman's body which, in actual practice, is, of course, very variable.

A is the wicket-keeper's original position on the off side of the wicket, from which he can see anything pitch in area A.

N.B.—This includes the majority of balls which are of average length, and within a reasonable distance of the leg stump.

B is the wicket-keeper's position when he is half-way across to the leg side, from which he can only view area B.

C is his final position, which commands a view of areas A, B and C, leaving only the black area, which is always hidden.

This diagram is not drawn strictly to scale, but rather with a view to emphasizing the limitations of position B.

This is accentuated when keeping to bowlers bowling over the wicket to left-handers, and round to right-handers, and makes the taking of a ball on the leg side more difficult, as more ground has to be covered to see and take the ball.

There is one more point in connection with taking leg balls. The closer the ball is to the batsman's legs the more difficult it is to pick up.

It would appear, therefore, that the wider the ball is on the leg side the easier it should be to take. This is true up to a point only, as the distance to be covered from outside the off stump soon counteracts the greater clarity of vision.

Now it was stated that it is essential to pick up the sight of the ball after it has passed the batsman's legs. There is a ball, though, which arrives every now and again which has to be taken blind. Take, for instance, a half volley or, perhaps, a little over, the pitch of which is obscured by legs, body or bat, which turns from the off just enough to beat the bat and legs, missing the latter by the narrowest of margins. It comes sneaking round the legs at the last moment. A very experienced wicket-keeper can, and does, take this ball blind, because he knows the pace of the ball in the air and off the wicket. He guesses accurately where it must come if it does get past bat and legs, and, above all, his hands give naturally to the ball at the moment of impact, even though this impact has not been actually foreseen by his eyes. Even then there is an element of luck.

Balls on the leg side which pass outside the batsman's legs have now been dealt with. There is still, however, that unpleasant customer to consider which passes between the bat and the batsman's legs, and misses the leg stump. It is probably the most difficult ball of all to take. In most cases it should be possible to see it pitch, but its subsequent career must be almost totally obscured by bat and legs, and the time available after it has passed these obstructions is infinitesimal. It is a very similar case to the ball over or very adjacent to the wicket, but not quite, as a big off-break often comes through that way and misses the wicket quite easily. It demands, however, the same treatment—a quick eye and a determination never to assume that it must hit bat, wicket or leg. Its clean taking is again the mark of a high-class wicket-keeper.

Standing up or back.—All this chapter has been written

under the assumption that the wicket-keeper is standing up. For standing back there is nothing to add with regard to hands or feet. Everything that has been said holds good.

The whole difficulty of taking leg balls is, however, eliminated as the distance the wicket-keeper is standing back gives ample time to pick up the line of flight of the ball on the leg side, and it becomes immaterial whether he observes its pitch from the off or leg side, or whether he actually sees it pitch at all. There is seldom the occasion for the applause which is constantly heard given to a wicket-keeper taking the ball on the leg side standing back, as it is far easier than a great many balls on the off when standing up. They sometimes demand a certain amount of agility, but that is all.

The only question that does arise, though, is where to stand when standing back. The answer is: In a position where the ball will come to the hands at a nice height; that is to say, just above the knees. The distance from the stumps depends upon the type and state of the wicket, and the pace of the bowler, but, assuming that the wicket-keeper is a good one and he is not going to stand back to medium stuff, it will be a very considerable distance away, and only just in front of the slips.

On no account must the half-way position be adopted. It has all the disadvantages of standing up, and none of the advantages. It is never done in first-class cricket of course, but it is seen far too often in all other classes of cricket, and is a practice which should be universally condemned.

It may be as well to consider here what are the advantages and disadvantages of standing up or back. The advantages of standing up are material and moral.

Material.—(1) A method of dismissing a batsman is available, *i.e.*, stumping, which is not available when standing back.

(2) A wicket-keeper standing up, who is active and alert, saves a considerable number of short runs which he cannot do if he is back—balls, for instance, which are just patted a yard or two from the wicket.

(3) It increases the chance of a fieldsman being able to run a batsman out, as very often it is impossible for a wicket-keeper to get up in time to receive a quick throw in when a batsman attempts a " cheeky " run.

Moral.—To a certain indefinite extent a good wicket-keeper, standing close up to the wicket, is inclined to cramp the batsman's freedom. It gives him an added danger to consider and guard against, at any rate. Furthermore, there are a great many bowlers who prefer their wicket-keeper up. G. O. Allen used to say at one time that he could not find his length unless the wicket-keeper stood up for a few overs, which was generally very unpleasant for the wicket-keeper as he has always been a very fast bowler, which people have only recently realized.

On the other hand, moderate-paced bowlers have been known to tell their wicket-keeper to stand back so that the batsman may be led to believe that they *are* fast.

Furthermore, a wicket-keeper up is a general encouragement to the close-in fielders, who like to have him there ready to throw at.

The advantages of standing back are that there should very rarely be any byes or catches missed, and that the wicket-keeper is most unlikely to damage himself. There is one other small point, and that is, with the wicket-keeper back, his range is increased and first slip can stand a bit wider, and more ground is covered in the slip area.

The best thing to consider in arriving at a decision whether to stand up or back, is whether standing up is liable to result in injury or missed catches. The same type of bowling probably produces both, and if the bowling is fast enough, or rising sharply enough off the pitch to make it probable that either will occur, it is better to stand back. An injury, it should be remembered, in addition to being unpleasant for the wicket-keeper, is a grave disadvantage to his side.

Standing back relieves the wicket-keeper of a certain amount of mental strain because it is easier, but, at the same time, it entails considerably more physical fatigue. He has constantly to sprint up to the wicket to take a throw in, rising balls have reached their maximum elevation when they come to him, those that keep low are at their lowest, and the turning ball is at its widest, *e.g.*, an off-break pitching just outside the batsman's legs is well out of reach unless the wicket-keeper moves quickly.

Boys and inexperienced wicket-keepers may have to stand back in order to limit the number of byes. In a recent Eton *v.* Harrow match a winning score was allowed to accumulate in byes, and the wicket-keeper remained standing up. Admittedly the bowlers were most at fault, but even a first-class wicket-keeper should never be too proud to give the bowlers "best." Now and again the bowling may be too erratic, or the wicket may be such that a moderately fast bowler makes the ball fly and shoot, and, under these circumstances, even the good wicket-keeper is well advised to stand back and catch the catches and stop the byes.

At the same time there is a tendency nowadays for county wicket-keepers to stand back to some very moderate-paced stuff, which is a pity, as, apart from anything else, the game loses some of its spectacular interest. However, we have to remember that county wicket-keepers have never a day from May to September in which to rest a bruised hand.

The most historic example of standing up to fast bowling was provided in a Gentlemen *v.* Players' match, when H. Martyn stood up to N. A. Knox and W. Brearley, and took them quite easily on both sides of the wicket.

Photo: *Sport & General.*

PLATE 7. ENGLAND v. AUSTRALIA, 1934.
Bradman, caught Ames bowled Verity. Sutcliffe and Hammond at gully and slip.

CHAPTER IV.

CATCHING.

THERE is naturally little to say about the principle of catching other than that which has already been said on the subject of taking the ball.

It is far the most important part of wicket-keeping, as more catches are offered at the wicket than in any other position, including the slips, and a glance at any wicket-keeper's victims for the season will show that stumping is a secondary consideration. The only case in which they are even approximate is Ames' victims off Freeman.

The question is often asked as to whether a wicket-keeper can follow the ball off the bat. The answer is that he can if the batsman touches the ball playing forward, because he has, roughly, three yards in which to see the deviation caused by contact with the bat.

Even this, though, does not give him time to follow an excessive deviation with his hands, and the ball in that case should go to first slip. The danger here is that the wicket-keeper, in trying to take this ball, may just get the ball on the outside of his hands or obstruct first slip's vision, in either case spoiling the catch. The worst of it is that the better he sees the ball off the bat the more likely he is to do it, and it is only long experience which will tell him when to withdraw his hands and let it go for the slips.

Now, when a batsman touches the ball playing back, his bat is so near the wicket-keeper's hands—in the case of a cut it is practically touching—that the direction of the ball cannot possibly be followed. At the same time, the ball has not time to deviate very much before it reaches the hands, and any ball that is struck hard enough to be turned clear of the hands must go to slips. The most difficult one is the ball which is struck hard enough to avoid the middle of the hands, but not enough to avoid them altogether.

This is the one which the spectators hear struck, and the wicket-keeper is denounced in the Press for a bad miss. Spectators do not notice the dropping of an easy catch which has only just been touched, and has therefore undergone very little deviation.

It is certain that when a spectator has heard the sound of a catch offered at the wicket it must have been a difficult one.

Wicket-keepers nowadays are expected to catch everything that is offered. A first-class wicket-keeper who kept for the Gentlemen some years ago stated that in his day they were only expected to catch about one out of three. In catching at the wicket, like everything else, there is an element of luck.

A wicket-keeper may be keeping very well, and yet about the only two balls that fail to go into his hands may be catches, or *vice versa*, he may be taking the ball indifferently the whole day, but two or three catches will go right into the middle of his hands.

The best advice that can be given to the young or inexperienced wicket-keeper is not to worry if he misses a catch. Worry leads to a lack of concentration, and over anxiety to retrieve a mistake leads to a snatch and a stiffening of the hands, wrists and arms when that exciting " click " is heard. If he continues to observe the principles which have been explained in the previous chapters he will hold on to practically all the easy catches, and continual match practice and experience will soon lead him to catching a very fair proportion of the more difficult chances.

There are two types of catch—both hit on the inside edge of the bat—which are very difficult. One turned inwards by a straight bat is particularly so. It is seldom expected, and the ball is almost totally obscured by the bat. The other is cut down by a cross bat as used for cutting. If the ball is of normal height, and the wicket-keeper's fingers are in the proper position pointing down, this is a very nasty one, as the hands are not in a position to take a ball with a steep angle of descent. If, however, the ball has risen and the hands are in the Plate 2 (ii) position, it is not quite so bad, as the ball is cut down into the palm of the left hand and the right closes over it.

A catch should never be missed standing back, except under exceptional circumstances, such as a ball cut down and dropping short, or a very wide one on the leg, to which only one hand can be got, which cannot be made a certainty. There is considerable excuse, too, if the slips, as they sometimes do (and never should do), shout in unison when they hear the ball touch the bat and before it has reached the wicket-keeper's hands.

Nevertheless, the best wicket-keepers do occasionally put them down. Many will remember that great Australian stumper, Carter, missing the then Major Tennyson at Lords in the Test Match in 1921. A very easy one, straight into his hands, standing back. The batsman increased his score subsequently by some seventy odd runs. The incomparable Oldfield, too, missed one at Lords in 1934 to everyone's amazement.

There is one other form of catch at the wicket, and that is the misshit or "skier." This should never be missed by a wicket-keeper if he can get his hands underneath it, as the spin on a misshit ball, which makes it liable to slip out of a fieldsman's hands, has no effect on gloves, and his hands are, in any case, twice the size.

It should be a recognized thing that the wicket-keeper takes any "skier" that he can get to. (See plate 7.) He should shout "Right" himself directly he sees that he can get under it, and should not even wait for his captain to call. Apart from everything else, his captain is not always in a position to do so. There was, however, in a recent 'Varsity match the spectacle of the Cambridge captain at first slip, with his wicket-keeper standing back, taking a skier himself and dropping it. It was a difficult one for a fieldsman as it was high and spinning, but the wicket-keeper must have caught it.

CHAPTER V.

STUMPING.

YOUNG and inexperienced wicket-keepers, and even some who have kept wicket for years, should try and forget that such a thing as stumping exists. Undue anxiety to remove the bails with the maximum celerity is the direct cause of all snatching, and in consequence of failure to take the ball, of a chance of stumping missed, or even more often of a catch being missed when the batsman has never even left his ground.

For stumping purposes the ball should be taken exactly as for catching. Once this is done the removal of the bails in the minimum of time is a simple matter. A boy of sixteen can remove the bails just as quickly as Ames provided he has taken the ball properly timed in his hands, is properly balanced on his feet, and his position in relation to the wicket is correct. Remember that in stumping the foot nearest the wicket does not move from the position it was in when the ball entered the hands. It acts unconsciously as a guide to the wicket for the hands, it *assumes the weight of the body*, and, if necessary, draws the other foot inwards. (See plate 8.) It is quite certain that if a chance of stumping is missed by slowness in removing the bails after the wicket-keeper has apparently taken the ball, that, either the ball has not been taken cleanly in his hands, or that his feet are in such a position that he is momentarily off his balance.

The question arises as to how the wicket-keeper knows when the batsman has left or is about to leave his ground, when presumably both eyes are concentrated on the ball. It is really rather a curious thing that a wicket-keeper is never unaware that a batsman has left his ground, even if he has only just dragged his toe on to the line.

The answer to this is that the wicket-keeper's vision does include a general view of the batsman as well as a concentrated view of the ball, and he gets to know almost by instinct what stroke played to what ball is liable to make the batsman leave his ground or lift his foot. The ball once taken is then transferred to the

Photo: *Central Press Photos, Ltd.*

PLATE 8. ENGLAND *v*. AUSTRALIA, 1934.
Hammond, stumped Oldfield bowled Grimmett.
A good example of off-side stumping.

Photo: Central Press Photos, Ltd.

PLATE 8. ENGLAND v. AUSTRALIA, 1934.

Hammond stumped Oldfield bowled Grimmett. A good example of off-side stumping. (Taken from a different angle.)

wicket and the bails whipped off. Very often the bails are not taken off, as it is obvious that it has been a false alarm, but the ball is there right against the wicket in case the batsman overbalances from the forward stroke that he has played. Very often a mistake is made, and the bails are, and should be, whipped off when the batsman is in his ground, as it has certainly appeared that he was going to leave his crease. But here it must be said that the practice of continually taking off the bails should be severely discouraged. It is unnecessary and theatrical; it encourages snatching, and it gives a lot of trouble to the umpire (often an old professional wicket-keeper), who, at any rate, has to make a gesture of coming up to put the bails on.

The spectacle of a wicket-keeper taking the bails off when a batsman has both feet firmly rooted in the crease is nearly always the sign of a moderate wicket-keeper. There are too many to be seen in club cricket. They are rated very smart by the spectators, whereas they are, in fact, inveterate snatchers, whose one idea of wicket-keeping is to remove the bails. Every young wicket-keeper passes through a phase of it, and the sooner he passes it the better. If he does not get out of it very quickly he never will—it will become a habit.

There is more excuse for taking the bails off unnecessarily on the leg side than on the off. This is due to two causes. One is that a batsman playing a ball on the leg is very apt to take his foot out of the crease after and not while he is playing the stroke. This is a question of balance and weight of the body, which need not be considered here. The other cause is that the wicket-keeper is so concerned in picking up the flight of the ball that his eyes do not observe the movement of the batsman to the same extent as on the off side.

It is, needless to say, a fatal mistake to glance deliberately at the batsman to see where his feet have got to. It is done sometimes though to a slow bowler, with the invariable result that the ball is fumbled. A fieldsman sometimes looks at the wicket he is going to throw at or the running batsman before the ball is in his hand, and he always fails to pick it up under these circumstances. It is a fault which is unlikely to occur with a fastish or even medium-paced bowler, as the quicker arrival of the ball does not allow time for the eyes to wander, but it does occur with slow bowlers, and must be guarded against.

Spectators are apt to imagine that the farther the batsman is out of his ground the easier is the chance of stumping. This is not always the case. Two or three inches is all that is required to give time to get the bails off, and if the batsman has gone out two or three yards he has probably got almost to the pitch of the ball, and has blinded the stumper's vision very completely.

"Good heavens; what a chance! He was yards out of his ground" is, however, the general comment. (See plate 9.)

The most difficult ball to stump off is the high, rising ball. In the first place, a downward motion of the hands is a slow and awkward movement compared to a sideways or upwards movement. In the second place, if Chapter II is remembered, the ball is taken in one hand, and that is the hand farthest removed from the wicket.

The quickest way is to transfer the ball to the underneath hand—that is the hand nearest the wicket—and remove the bails with one hand. There is undoubtedly a slight delay in this method, but it is a delay that should not prove fatal unless the batsman is back in his crease very quick. In any case, it is quicker than bringing the hand down which has taken the ball, the fingers of which, it will be remembered, are perpendicular.

There are two methods of stumping off a very wide ball. One is to move both feet across in the ordinary way, take the ball, if possible, in the inside hand, and remove the bails with one hand. Both hands will not reach if the ball is very wide. If the ball has not been taken in the inside hand it can be quickly transferred, as in the case of a rising ball, and there is a very slight delay, which again should not prove fatal.

The other method is to keep the inside leg near enough to the wicket to ensure that it will be possible to reach the wicket with both hands, and to put the outside leg at full stretch, take the ball, and sweep both hands to the wicket.

The latter method is the easier and quicker way of stumping, but it is more likely to lead to a missed catch. Remember a batsman jumping out to a leg-break bowler pitching one outside the off stump is very apt to "tickle" it.

Photo: *Sport & General.*]

PLATE 9. ENGLAND *v.* AUSTRALIA, 1930.
"Good Heavens—What a chance!" Ponsford escapes.

PLATE 10. ENGLAND v. AUSTRALIA, 1934.
Ames takes a wide throw to try to run out Chipperfield.

Photo: *Sport & General*]

CHAPTER VI.

Running Out.

This is a department of the game in which a wicket-keeper is dependent upon the co-operation of his colleagues, the fieldsmen.

His—the wicket-keeper's—part is to take up a position close behind the stumps, and directly facing the fieldsman who is throwing. Having done this he must pray for a decent throw in, and remember not to snatch at it. Now, in running out, the footwork should be similar to the second method suggested in Chapter V for the stumping off a wide ball, *i.e.*, the inside foot must remain very close to the wicket, and must not follow the outside foot any distance. (See plate 10.) This often does not allow the hands to be in the position advocated in the general principles, but it must be remembered that the vision of the ball is not obstructed in running out, and, furthermore, there is no chance of deviation by the bat at the last moment. The actual reception of the ball in the hands should therefore be easy, and the only thing that remains to be done is to bring the hands to the wicket in the minimum of time. This is ensured by keeping the inside foot close to the wicket.

If a throw is out of reach of such a position, the wicket-keeper must go to it, take it in the hand nearest the wicket and step back again, reaching for the wicket with that hand. Never give up hope due to a wide, bad throw. The overthrows have got to be saved by someone, and there may be time to get the batsman out.

What is a decent throw in? There are only two: a full pitch or a long hop, not more than an inch or two higher than the top of the stumps. Once they get higher than that there is the downward movement of the hands necessary, which can never be so quick as the upwards or sideways.

A full pitch needs a little more give of the hands than any other ball probably, as in most cases it is quicker through the air than a long hop is off the turf, but its consequent earlier arrival at the wicket more than compensates for any time lost in allowing this extra "give."

The trouble is that it is difficult to get a really good full pitch. A long hop allows a much greater margin of error in the trajectory, and should not normally strike bad turf and bounce false, unless it is thrown from close to the wicket, when a full pitch should always be employed.

Half-volleys and yorkers are, in addition to their obvious difficulties, very liable to do this as they pitch in the neighbourhood of block holes and bowlers' footmarks.

This is not the place to discuss the subject of throwing in as it is the fieldsman's department, but there is no doubt that the general standard of throwing in England is moderate in all classes of cricket, and adds greatly to the anxieties and fatigue of a wicket-keeper.

All he can do is to remember always to be ready, and encourage a throw in from any part of the field. Never let him be seen looking away when any fieldsman has the ball, even if there is no chance of a run.

There is a great deal to be said in favour of fieldsmen (except mid off and mid on) always returning the ball to the wicket-keeper. In the first place, the ball is "killed" and no over-throws can result. A bowler often has a shorter throw, and bowlers should not throw unnecessarily. It is good practice for all fieldsmen, and, finally, the bowler has a much better chance of getting the ball returned to him as a nice easy catch. It is an essential part of a wicket-keeper's job to return the ball to the bowler as a nice easy catch. It should not be thrown high up in the air so that he has to wait for it, and possibly look up into the sun. On the other hand, it should not be thrown hard, or, more important, low enough to make him bend. Something between the two is required. It is not so easy to do, especially when standing right back to a fast bowler, who often starts walking back preparatory to delivering the next ball, looking over his shoulder, and then grumbling if he does not get an accurate throw.

There is one throw which presents a difficulty, and that is a ball very close to the wicket, even if it is the long hop or full pitch. The wicket itself may obstruct a final vision of the ball, and the excessive proximity of the wicket-keeper's hands to the wicket may put him off, even granted that he does not make the error of assuming that the ball is going to hit the wicket. It is not a bad plan if it is obviously going to be a very close thing to take half a step back from the wicket, so as to be able to take the ball, say, a foot behind the wicket.

When standing back it must be remembered that in order to take a throw in and run a man out when attempting a sharp single it is necessary to start up to the wicket immediately the ball is played. Sometimes even then the wicket-keeper arrives too late to get in a position to take the ball, and nothing is more irritating to the fielder concerned and to the captain and to all the other fielders.

It should be remembered, too, that if the wicket-keeper is not in position when the fieldsman picks up the ball he almost invariably throws a yorker at the bottom of the stumps, or tries to do so. It is a natural thing to do, and appears to give a greater margin of error. This is a difficult one to take in any case, and almost impossible if the wicket-keeper arrives running from ten or twelve yards back.

CHAPTER VII.

Byes.

Byes are the only part of extras over which the wicket-keeper has any control, though he is often blamed for a large score of extras in which possibly leg-byes or no-balls have played the major part. The number of byes let by a wicket-keeper in the course of a match seldom has a direct bearing on the result, but they must, of course, be kept down to the absolute minimum. They may possibly have an effect upon the result—they have a moral effect, and it must be remembered that someone, very often a bowler fielding at slip, has to run to the boundary after them.

On some wickets, and with some bowlers, it is difficult to prevent a certain number being given away, and the number of byes in a score sheet is seldom a just criterion of how well or how badly a wicket-keeper has performed. At the same time, a performance like Oldfield's, who, in the first four completed innings played by England in 1928—1929, conceded only three byes out of 1923 runs, must denote a really high-class wicket-keeper.

The taking of chances is a wicket-keeper's first care, and the stopping of byes a secondary consideration. If, however, he is always in a position to take his chances, he automatically stops the byes, more especially as his pads automatically become his second line of defence, and they should, and do, stop the majority of balls which he has failed to take with his hands. The better the wicket-keeper the fewer balls will fail to go into his hands, but watch a really high-class wicket-keeper for an afternoon and it will be seen that a certain number of balls hit his pads, without any deliberate intention on his part. It will be noticed that they are, in most cases, the balls which keep very low. A young wicket-keeper should never be allowed to put his pads in the way deliberately to stop a ball. After a lot of experience a wicket-keeper does get to know a difficult ball that may evade his hands, and makes a special effort to bring his second line of defence into play, or, rather, to make additionally sure that it is there. But it should not be encouraged in the young because it so easily is allowed to become their chief line of defence.

The majority of byes that are conceded in all classes of cricket are on the leg side. The obvious difficulty of these balls has already been explained in the chapter on taking the ball as due to the obstruction of vision caused by the batsman's body. This is magnified by lack of experience and nerve, but even the best wicket-keepers will let byes off erratic leg-bowling, though they are perfectly able to deal all day with a bowler who is bowling an organized leg theory.

Other types of balls likely to result in byes are:—The balls very close to the wicket, expecially between the batsman's legs and the wicket. Their difficulty has already been explained. The good length ball which " flies " or rises abruptly. The natural and, indeed, necessary movement, is to get the head out of the line of the ball, and the hands follow. Lastly, the ball which swings wide and keeps low. This is not so bad when it is short, but, when a good length or over, it is very unpleasant, as the wicket-keeper has little time to get down to it. Such a ball is, if missed by the wicket-keeper, often within reach of first slip, but it comes very quick to him, and a great many slips seem unwilling to put a hand to a ball of this nature which has not been touched by the bat.

As a general rule, the lower the total score the higher will be the percentage of byes, because it will mean that the bowlers have been making the ball do things. It is impossible, however, to form a judgment from the score sheet. How often has one gone to see a particular wicket-keeper perform, and he only has a few simple balls to take during the entire afternoon. There are other occasions, though, when he may be severely tested for hours on end.

Taking all sorts of wickets and bowling throughout a season, a wicket-keeper does all right if he only concedes 4 per cent. of the total in byes. Say that runs are scored at the rate of one a minute, it means that he lets one ball past him every hour and forty minutes, or three or four in a full day's play.

CHAPTER VIII.

APPEALING.

APPEALING is a job which a wicket-keeper shares with a bowler, and both are liable to opprobrium because of it on some occasions. Too much appealing is an undesirable habit. It naturally incurs the resentment of the opposing side, and also of the spectators.

On the other hand, a wicket-keeper must remember that the bowler often has run so wide after the delivery of a ball that he is not in a position to appeal for l.b.w., and that the wicket-keeper owes it to his side to appeal if there is any chance of a batsman being in the wrong.

To the casual cricket spectator it would seem that the wicket-keeper should be as good a judge as the umpire of an l.b.w. appeal, but this is not the case, as the modern batsman, at any rate, plays a great many straight balls with his legs in such a position that the wicket-keeper cannot see the ball pitch (though he knows that it must have pitched on the wicket). When these hit the batsman's legs the wicket-keeper is very apt to appeal, as he is unable to tell what the ball has done at the last moment, either in the air or off the pitch. It may have hit a portion of the batsman's pads at such an angle that it had no chance of hitting the wicket, or, on the other hand, it may have come straight through and the batsman is out. Remember that the bowler has run wide, and that he relies on his wicket-keeper to assist him in all appeals, and so do not blame the latter if occasionally he asks for a bad one.

At the same time, there are a great many balls which the bowler naturally appeals for, and which, in some cases, are given out, which the wicket-keeper knows well are not going to hit the wicket. Probably the majority of these are the ones which are going over the top.

As regards catches at the wicket, the batsman is the best qualified judge whether the ball has been struck, except under the circumstances when he strikes his pad or the ground with his bat as well as the ball. These are not very rare circumstances, and lead to the batsman swearing that he only hit his pad or the ground, whereas the wicket-keeper knows that he hit the ball.

Under all other circumstances, the batsman feels the touch of the ball on the bat or glove, but, naturally, the concussion of the bat and pad, or bat and ground, is the greater and eliminates the minor one.

The next best judge is the wicket-keeper, and the umpire a bad third. The wicket-keeper's two chief difficulties are, first, to distinguish between pad and bat on the leg side. In this case he has obviously had a very bad sight of the ball, but even then the ball comes into the hands quicker and sharper off the bat, and is generally distinguishable from the pad. Secondly, a very slight touch off a half-volley when, as is very often the case, the ground is struck at practically the same moment as the ball enters the hand. The noise of the bat on the ground is inseparable from the noise of the ball on the bat, and is apt to confuse if the ball is so slightly touched that the spin imparted to it is not felt in the hands.

The umpire is there, after all, to be asked his opinion on the subject, and as long as the question is not presented in too offensive a manner the wicket-keeper is fully justified in appealing for a good many cases in which the decision is, rightly, in the batsman's favour.

In first-class cricket in England, the umpires are so good that no one is going to be "jockeyed" out by over-appealing.

In fact, it is the reverse, and the more bad appeals are made the more likely the batsman is to get away with a decision that might, under other circumstances, have gone against him.

In club cricket in England, umpires are only human and apt to bow to the *force majeure*, and, with due regard to what has been said in this chapter, appeals should be as limited as possible.

In the Colonies and other countries umpires are mostly poor, but honest: poor through lack of experience. Unnecessary appeals are apt to rattle them and produce wrong decisions, both for and against the applicants, which may or may not be in equal proportion, but which are sure to lead to ill-feeling and mutual recriminations.

CHAPTER IX.

Care and Remedies for the Hands.

A WICKET-KEEPER'S first care is for his hands. They are as valuable to him as are the legs of a ballet dancer. The slightest injury to them may make him useless. Every ball insists upon hitting the injured part, and even if it does not he always thinks that it is going to do so, and there is an involuntary flinching, a loss of nerve, and a performance which in no way resembles his best form. Furthermore, an injury often results in his having to retire in the middle of the game, which places his side at a very severe disadvantage, and if, as is generally the case, there is only a very inadequate substitute renders the attack a farce.

There is only one way to reduce to a minimum the chances of injury to the hands, and that is by correct taking of the ball, as laid down in Chapter II.

Any form of snatching or the "rat-trap" method of catching a ball must obviously result in injured fingers.

But even perfect taking of the ball cannot entirely eliminate the risk of accident, especially to the fingers.

The most usual part of the hand (as apart from the fingers) to suffer is the palm, just below the first, second and third fingers. This is, of course, due to bad timing of the ball and insufficient "give" of the hands. It is most likely to occur in keeping on a fast wicket for the first time in a season. Some people's hands are much more tender in that particular place than others, and it must be remembered that it is the one place where the padding of a glove cannot be overdone.

The only real cure is rest, combined with any ordinary method of taking out a bruise, the best of which is probably to soak the hand in very hot water, mixed with arnica and soda. *Do not rub any bruise, either in the palm of the hand or on the fingers.*

The rest of the palm is well padded, both by nature and in the gloves, and should not suffer. The wrists, too, are extremely well protected by good gloves.

To prevent bruising of the palms, and in order to carry on if a bruise had occurred, it used to be the custom to use raw meat inside the gloves. A thin slice would form a fairly adequate protection, but it was disgustingly messy, and has long since given way to plasticine or strips of absorbent sponge. The latter is probably the better protection, but it is the more bulky of the two, and plasticine moulds itself into the shape of the hands and takes up very little room in the glove. If the bruise is not widespread, however, a corn-plaster cut in two and stuck not on, but on each side of the sore place, is probably the best of all.

The thumbs are rather liable to blows, especially from balls struck fairly hard by the bat, or very often a ball hitting a wicket or a ball rising sharply. Mercifully, they are well endowed by nature to withstand rough treatment, being short and strong. The top joint can only suffer a bruise: it is normally too strong for any form of dislocation, though it has been known to occur. The bottom joint may become sprained. This is painful, but not so serious as it sounds, as that joint can be strapped so tightly in adhesive plaster that it cannot move at all.

There is no necessity for the thumb to move from that joint, and there is plenty of room there in the glove to take the strapping, which should encircle the joint in layers and extend down to the wrist.

We now come to injuries of the fingers. There is the common bruise, for which rest, if possible, and some form of fomentation, as described above, is the remedy.

There is the bruise of the joint, which is more troublesome and deep-seated, and probably will require radiant heat, and there is injury to the joints caused by the ball being received on the end of the finger. The outward result of this is apparently the same as a bruise caused by direct blows on the joint, but it is very important to remember that in these cases there are always displacements of the little tendons and ligaments which run down on each side of the joints. This is not a medical treatise, but let it be sufficient to say that a finger will be painful for a very long time, and will remain permanently enlarged unless these tendons or ligaments are put back into place. An ordinary practitioner will merely prescribe heat or electrical treatment, which will, of course, take down the inflammation, but nothing else. Incidentally, the best form of electrical treatment for either sprain or bruise is that which, after the injured part has been well "baked," drives iodine through the skin.

In any case of an injured joint some form of bone-setter should be consulted, a man who makes a business of small tendons and their relation to bones. In one minute, with a slight click or two, he will have got them back into place, and the finger will soon become normal.

The complete dislocation of a finger joint, of course, requires medical treatment, fomentation to take out the inflammation, and probably a short period of rest. Very often, though, they are less troublesome than the injury described above, simply because, in the latter case, the dislocation of small tendons and ligaments is merely treated as a bruise.

Any form of break, of course, involves a splint and a long rest.

The question of providing additional protection for fingers that have suffered is a difficult one, as there is not room in the glove for much extra padding, or anything of that nature. Remember, never put strapping round an injured finger; it stops the circulation, and after about half an hour intensifies any pain.

Quite the best thing to get made and have always at hand are one or two aluminium finger splints. A surgical manufacturer will make them for a small price. They should be a fraction of an inch longer than the finger, so that they take a blow on the end of the finger. Two sizes will probably do. They are shaped in a groove so that the finger lies inside, and is protected practically on three sides. They should, when required, be strapped with adhesive plaster on to the inner glove, so that the base is just where the finger joins the hand. If any form of finger tip is removed from that particular finger it will be found that they slip easily into the outer glove and form a most excellent protection. They permit, of course, no flexion of the top or middle joint, but it will be found that in the case of one or even two fingers that does not effect the necessary gripping power.

Apart from correct taking of the ball, the best preventive of injury to the fingers is to strap them up with adhesive plaster whenever keeping wicket. Start just above the top joint, and strap to just above the middle joint. Some wicket-keepers include the middle joint, but this is apt to limit gripping power too much till the plaster works loose, when it becomes useless. Furthermore, the middle joints are stronger, further removed from a blow on the end of the finger, and less liable to suffer injury. The plaster serves a two-fold purpose. It forms an additional padding, which is not bulky, and it gives strong support to the joint, and helps it to resist any form of dislocation which might be caused by a blow on the end of the finger.

It is a great nuisance to do this, especially if going out for ten minutes only at the end of the day; but it is with a new ball that accurate taking is sometimes most difficult, and it is well worth it every time. There is no adhesive plaster which does not leave dirty marks on the fingers which soap will not remove. A little petrol, however, will take them off in a minute; failing that, it can be done in five minutes with pumice stone.

It is really amazing how seldom professional wicket-keepers are out of action through damaged hands as compared with amateurs, and it probably proves the statement of an old professional wicket-keeper that "All amateurs snap 'em a bit."

CHAPTER X.

Equipment.

The choice of gloves is always a difficult problem, as there are several very good makes on the market at the present time.

The chief difference between the various types is that some have short fingers and some long, and that some have more padding in them than others.

As regards the fingers, a wicket-keeper must find out by experience which shape of glove suits his hands best and make the best " cup " in which to receive the ball.

There has got to be a certain amount of padding somewhere, and it does not make much difference really whether it is in the outer glove or the inner. The great thing to remember, though, is that there should be the minimum amount of padding, consistent with saving the hands from bruising. The ball will bounce out of an over-padded glove, particularly if there is too much padding at the top of the palm, as this does not permit of a cup being formed to receive the ball. Too tight a glove has a similar effect, and must be guarded against.

As regards inner gloves, a pair of what are known as "boy's wicket-keeping gloves" are probably the best. Why a boy should not have a proper pair of outer gloves it is difficult to say, but these are unrubbered gloves made of soft leather in the " gauntlet " shape.

Provided the outer glove has a certain amount of padding this should be sufficient, but if it has not, it will probably be necessary to wear a pair of chamoix leather gloves as well under the boy's gloves.

It should be remembered that padding of both outer and inner gloves get less effective after continual use, and a spare pair of chamoix leather gloves should always be in a wicket-keeper's bag as a reinforcement if and when this should occur.

There is one other thing to consider, and that is the type of finger tip to be used. There are two types of finger tip, both made of stiff leather, which gets softer with use. One long type extends practically the whole length of the finger. When new, these must necessarily be stiff, effect the gripping power of the fingers, and tend to make the ball bounce out of the hand. To many people they seem clumsy, even when old and soft, but, nevertheless, they offer good protection to the fingers, and are used by a certain amount of wicket-keepers. The short tips are similar, except that they only cover the top joints of the fingers. These are probably the most used.

A small piece of absorbent sponge in the top of each tip is an excellent thing, as it greatly minimizes the concussion of a ball striking the end of the finger, and it is these balls that do the damage. Lastly, there is the rubber finger tip, which is only just large enough for the tip of each finger to rest in, and which has sufficient thickness of rubber to minimize a blow on the end of the finger. If plaster is always used to strap the top joints these are probably the best of all, but the average glove does not have sufficient padding in the fingers to protect the top joints without the use of strapping or the leather tips.

The surface of the wicket-keeper's gloves is a constant source of worry. If nothing is done to them they get as slippery as ice, and once preparations are used to improve the surface they get sticky, and the bowler has a very righteous grievance. At all costs avoid spoiling the new ball by having too much stuff on the gloves. The shine on a new ball is often worth two quick wickets and the match. Furthermore, it is generally a fast bowler who is entrusted with the new ball, and fast bowlers seem by nature more temperamental than others and more likely to complain violently of little incidents like that, which may jeopardize the chances of getting an early wicket.

The rubber facing of gloves perishes very quickly in any case, and any form of dressing makes them do so much quicker. Eucalyptus oil is probably the least harmful, but its smell is very strong, and it requires constant application, as it evaporates very quickly.

Any form of resin invariably becomes too sticky sooner or later, and is immediate ruination to the gloves, as the rubber is pulled off in great strips whenever the gloves are put together. They stick to the pads, bats and everything in the cricket bag, and are a general nuisance and anxiety. Even if the desired stickiness has been arrived at for one match there is no guarantee that if they have been left in the sun, or even in the cricket bag in a warm room, that they will not be a glue-pot the next day.

Probably the best treatment for a pair of new rubber-faced gloves—and no perfect treatment has yet been discovered—is to give them three or four good rubbings with a mixture of eucalyptus oil and neatsfoot oil. This should produce a surface which is more or less permanent, but which can be improved from time to time by the application of a very small quantity of any ordinary bat oil, which is available in any pavilion. The gloves should be well rubbed together till the oil has disappeared, and it will be found that the rubber has been resoftened and the slightly rough surface of the rubber revived. This is much the quickest and easiest treatment, especially for the club cricketer, who probably arrives on the ground with little time to spare, and possibly has not inspected his bag since the previous Saturday.

It should be remembered that gloves can easily be refaced in a short time and at a small cost, so that, provided they last through a season, the deterioration of the rubber is not of great importance.

Crepe-faced gloves have comparatively recently been brought on the market. They certainly have great advantages, in that they wear well and need practically no treatment, as they always carry a rough surface. When perfected, they will probably entirely supersede the old rubber face. At present the crepe is too thick and stiff, and does not form a nice cup when the hand is bent. It is apt to get hard (though not slippery), when it tends to make the ball bounce out.

If used, care should be taken not to leave them in a hot sun for long, as they are apt to turn into glue. If a thinner, softer type of crepe could be evolved, it would probably make a perfect facing.

It is advisable always to carry a spare pair of gloves in the cricket bag. Borrowed gloves are impossible to "keep" in, and some accident may always occur to one pair.

It should not be necessary to have enormous special wicket-keeping pads, which must tend to clumsy footwork, and to lack of mobility when standing back, in running for a skier or short run. In these days of pad play all pads afford good protection. A wicket-keeper, though, should be very careful to see that the pieces of cross-padding on the inside have not got thin and flat by use, and that the padding in the neighbourhood of the knee has not suffered in a similar manner. This is most important, as it is a most likely place to be struck on and most vulnerable.

It should hardly be necessary to say that no one should ever keep wicket without a protector, and that special care should be taken to see that it is comfortable, as the continual bending up and down of the wicket-keeper is much more liable to make it shift than running when batting. An "athletic slip" worn under the protector greatly increases its comfort and efficiency.

CHAPTER XI.

WICKET-KEEPING AND BATTING.

THE question is often asked why are wicket-keepers never good batsmen, and a satisfactory answer has never been given. It is not quite correct to say that they never are good batsmen, but in the highest class of cricket it is a fact that they are very few and far between.

Some years ago William Storer was the outstanding example of the wicket-keeper batsman. He kept wicket for England superbly, and was selected to play for The Players on his batting alone. From the time when Storer was in his prime, getting on for forty years ago, until the present day, there was no wicket-keeper batsman of the highest class in both departments.

There is now Leslie Ames, who, if not quite the best wicket-keeper in England, is not very far off it, and who would almost certainly be selected to play for England on his batting alone. Incidentally, it is not everyone who knows that Ames is a magnificent fielder, especially in the deep.

When Ames went out to Australia with Jardine's team in 1932-33 it was generally anticipated that he would enhance his reputation as a batsman rather than as a wicket-keeper. As it turned out, he kept wicket admirably in all the Test Matches, but gave a disappointing display with the bat, which tends to show that it is very difficult to do both—in high-class cricket at any rate.

The most outstanding example of a wicket-keeper batsman, however, is H. B. Cameron, of South Africa. He is, at this time, second only to Oldfield in the world's wicket-keepers, and would undoubtedly be selected to play for his country on batting alone. Many people would here mention Alfred Lyttleton, but it must be remembered that he "kept" in the days of long-stops, and also was never subjected to the many days in the field, which are the lot of the more modern wicket-keeper.

It would seem that a wicket-keeper has exceptional opportunities to become a good batsman. He should go in already set if he has been watching the ball off the

[Photo: *Sport & General*.]

PLATE 11. ENGLAND v. SOUTH AFRICA, 1929.
Cameron 'keeping behind Sutcliffe.

pitch for half the day. He knows the light, the pace of the wicket; in fact, everything. He is constantly watching the best batsman at very close quarters for hours at a time. He must have a very intimate knowledge of the tactics and wiles of every class of bowler, and he has a quickness of eye which enables him to see and pick up a ball when its flight has been practically or even wholly obstructed from his view. Surely nothing could be simpler than batting! Why is it that he is no good?

Some people suggest that once a wicket-keeper becomes a good enough bat to get a place in a decent side he naturally gives up the dangerous and thankless task of wicket-keeping.

There may be a substratum of truth in this jest, because there are every year a few very good schoolboy wicket-keeper batsmen. How many leave the 'Varsity as such? They probably find one day, after making some runs, that they have to go straight out and keep wicket; they do not do quite so well as usual. Possibly they have made runs in both innings, and are on the field of play during a very large proportion of a three-day match. Hitherto they have only had to bat and keep wicket at the most for two days in the week. Their wicket-keeping is probably the first to suffer; they are a little bit tired really, though they do not notice it, but their power of concentration fails somewhat. A wicket-keeper who has no ideas of batting is tried in his place, and does much better. The wicket-keeper batsman is probably played for batting alone in the next match, finds it is an easier life, and gradually gives up the wicket-keeping. *Vice versa*, if he has made some small scores, but kept wicket well, he says, "I can get into this side as a wicket-keeper," ceases to trouble about batting, and gradually is relegated to a number nine or ten position in the batting order. R. P. Lewis, who kept wicket for Oxford for three years, and subsequently for Surrey, is supposed not to have made an aggregate of 100 runs in first-class cricket. Someone, estimating his batting ability, said, "He backs up well."

This, however, does not quite explain why, say, the young professional, who gets his place in a County side as a wicket-keeper, should not develop his batting. Why, for instance, should Strudwick have been a number eleven all his life?

It may be that, being assured of a place in the County side, they just do not bother about anything else.

Nobody encourages them to do so. The captain, or Selection Committee, have arranged their team so that a wicket-keeper and two or three bowlers should form the inevitable tail, and as long as they do their particular job, and perhaps occasionally defy the bowling for half an hour, all is well.

Some theoretical reasons are advanced, such as that a wicket-keeper gets so accustomed to focus the ball coming into his hands that he is unable to get the correct focus to hit it two or three yards further away; that the footwork and balance on the feet is quite different; that his hands, from constant concussion, lose the more sensitive grip of the bat, which is essential to perfect timing and other theories of this nature.

If an answer can be given to this question, it is probably that a good batsman has no need to, and never takes up, wicket-keeping. That a good wicket-keeper never feels that it is encumbent upon him to take up batting, and that a good wicket-keeper batsman, once he reaches first-class matches and three-day cricket, finds the strain begins to tell, and speedily relinquishes one or the other. Coming to International cricket, the strain is doubled and trebled, and when we consider the concentrated hours on the field of play, which would be the lot of a wicket-keeper who made runs in both innings in a six-day match in Australia, it is small wonder that there are very few exceptions to prove the rule.

Cameron and Ames, the two present-day exceptions, are of a very equable temperament and men of iron.

CHAPTER XII.

BOWLERS AND WICKETS.

No wicket-keeper can attain a high standard unless he studies the various types of bowlers with whom he is likely to be confronted.

The county wicket-keeper has an enormous advantage in this respect as he has five or six bowlers for whom he " keeps " the whole summer, and he knows exactly what they are trying to do and only has to guard against the vagaries of English turf.

Bowlers divide themselves into four general classes—fast, swerve, seam, and spin bowlers. Fast bowlers need little study—there is only the problem to be settled as to whether to stand up or back. In most cases they swing the new ball a little and, when the shine is off, turn the ball a little from the off.

Swing bowlers naturally lose a certain amount of their swing as the ball gets old, but there are many who can still make the ball do a bit in the air even when the ball is old. They are divided into two classes—the out-swinger and the in-swinger. The out-swinger should present few difficulties to the wicket-keeper, and, at the same time, produce a certain number of catches. The right-handed in-swinger is a comparatively modern production—the late T. A. Jacques of Hampshire, and B. G. Von Melle, the South African, who, when at Oxford, was top of the first-class bowling averages, were the earliest well-known exponents of this art shortly before the war.

A late in-swinger is one of the hardest balls a wicket-keeper has to deal with—he can never be sure that it is going to swing, and if it is directed on the middle or leg stump it suddenly jerks out of sight, pitches on the blind spot and has whistled past the batsman's legs before the wicket-keeper has time to get across, and even if he has done so it is most awkward to pick up its flight.

It is very important though, to be able to deal with it, as it is a ball that a batsman is likely to touch, or he may take his right foot out of his ground in attempting to glide.

The seam bowler is comparatively simple, as the change of direction of the ball can be watched off the pitch, and, furthermore, it is very slight, much slighter than a spun or swinging ball. Seam bowlers cut the ball with the middle finger and try to make it pitch on one or other side of the seam, which causes the ball to deviate two or three inches in either direction. This is enough to beat the bat, but should not be enough to worry the wicket-keeper. It is no good trying to anticipate which way it is going to turn off the pitch, as it is very difficult to tell the bowler's intention from his hand, and the ball very often does not do what it is intended to in this class of bowling. Seam bowlers are top-spin bowlers and, consequently, get additional pace off the pitch, *e.g.*, Tate. Swing bowlers are, of course, seam bowlers, too, and swing and seam (as described above) are often combined.

The ordinary spin bowler's intention should be obvious from careful attention to his hand. By ordinary spin bowling we mean the right-handed bowler, who bowls leg and off break, or both, and the left hander, who, when he spins the ball, bowls a leg break to the batsman. The plain, off spinner offers comparatively few chances to the wicket-keeper and probably relies on short legs or l.b.ws., by bowling round the wicket. Any form of leg break is obviously going to give the wicket-keeper a good many chances of getting his name on the score sheet.

Now, the googly bowler is a spin bowler who presents much more difficulty. He bowls the leg break, the googly, *i.e.*, the off break with leg break action, and the top spinner which goes straight through. Unless the wicket-keeper is certain of the googly bowler's intentions, by careful study of his hand, it is impossible to " keep " properly to this class of bowler. Some are harder to detect than others, but there are no googly bowlers who can often deceive their regular wicket-keeper, though Bosanquet bowled Lilley with a " wrong un " in a Gentlemen *v.* Players match just after Lilley had been " keeping " to him in Australia. G. T. S. Stevens is probably the most difficult of the present-day googly bowlers to detect.

If a wicket-keeper finds that he is going to " keep " for a strange googly bowler he should get him in the net before the match and endeavour to spot it. He may have to resort to a signal, but this is very unsatisfactory as it may be forgotten by the bowler, and the wicket-keeper is then worse off than before, or it may be detected by the batsman.

Even granted that the wicket-keeper knows his bowler well, this type of bowling is still difficult since the googly itself is an " overspun " ball which turns a lot, gets a tremendous pace off the pitch in comparison to its pace in the air, and is very apt to rise very quickly off the pitch. A googly bowler and a quickish in-swinger are the two most difficult bowlers to " keep " to.

Having taken a quick survey of bowlers and their methods, which should be studied by all wicket-keepers, it will be as well to add a word about the types of wickets on which they bowl.

There is the plumb wicket, which may be fast or easy paced—the latter is the nicest, but is apt to offer few opportunities for the wicket-keeper to distinguish himself. The fast is easy, too, once its pace has been gauged, and offers a certain amount of opportunity, as a batsman, playing late on a ball, is apt to offer a catch, as well as if he plays inside a swinging or turning ball.

Then there is the slow dead wicket, which is also easy and apt to offer a few chances to the wicket-keeper. It gives opportunity for comparatively easy taking of the ball on the leg side, as the lack of pace off the pitch gives more time to pick up a sight of the ball.

There is the sticky wicket—difficult in every way, as if there is a bowler who can really spin the ball it turns very sharply *and* rises, or it may strike a piece of much wetter turf, fail to take the spin and cut through quick and low. Every other ball, too, comes through at a different pace.

Then there is the worn, hard wicket—the wicket which has probably started all right, but has lost its top surface. This is a terror to batsmen and wicket-keepers alike, as on it the ball produces all the tricks of a sticky wicket with a uniform but additional pace off the pitch. A sticky wicket is never fast, and a wicket-keeper has more time to follow the ball off the pitch than he does upon a worn, fast wicket.

Lastly, as far as grass is concerned, there is the definitely bad wicket—that is, bad turf. This, nowadays, is comparatively rarely met with except in village cricket, and as was said in Chapter I, should be avoided if possible, as if it does not lead to actual injury, it leads to loss of nerve and bad habits.

Finally, there are matting wickets, which are used in most parts of the world except England. They are used in places where it is difficult or impossible to grow grass which will make a suitable or lasting pitch. Sometimes the matting is laid on such grass as there is, sometimes it is laid on the bare soil or some mixture thereof, which has been prepared and rolled to make a hard, flat, smooth surface.

It would appear that there would be a vast difference between matting laid on grass and on bare soil. As a matter of fact there is little. Certainly, matting laid on grass is apt to produce a ball which is slightly slower and turns, perhaps, a little bit more, and in some cases is not quite so true in its bounce. But as far as the wicket-keeper is concerned they are much the same, but both are entirely different from a grass wicket. In the first place they take more spin. A fast bowler can turn the ball an unpleasant amount. Secondly, every ball rises at a much more acute angle off the pitch, and comes higher to the wicket-keeper. This is particularly the case of a ball which has been spun a lot. On matting wickets for instance, the googlies (which are over-spun balls) of bowlers such as Freeman or Peebles are more than likely to go over the top of the wicket.

All this sounds difficult, and does take time to get accustomed to. On the other hand, matting wickets are true and uniform, and the unexpected rarely, if ever, happens. A ball takes the spin which has been imparted to it, so much and no more, and does not deceive so often as on a grass wicket. For this reason it is additionally important for the wicket-keeper to study the bowler's fingers most carefully.

The ball is always on the rise, but except for a few overs with a new ball (or on a brand new mat, which should never be used) it does not " fly," *i.e.*, a good-length ball never gets up a dangerous height for no particular reason, and, above all, the " shooter " is practically unknown.

The chief advantage to the wicket-keeper, though, lies in the uniformity of pace. Matting never varies to any appreciable extent, and there is no question of " keeping " on a hard, fast wicket one day and on a slow, sticky one the next, or on a two-paced wicket.

CHAPTER XIII.

MAKING A YOUNG WICKET-KEEPER.

PARENTS, sometimes, not often, when deciding upon a cricketing career for their sons, wonder whether it is a good thing to try and make him a wicket-keeper.

Mother generally (if she knows anything at all about cricket) says " No, it is so dangerous, he might get hit in the face, and I don't want him to have his fingers knocked about like that Mr. Stumper who was staying here the other day." Father says, " I don't mind about that, but to get into the school eleven he has got to be the best wicket-keeper, whereas he can be the sixth or seventh best bat, and the fourth or fifth best bowler, and still get a place."

Mother's argument need not be considered, and father's is no better, as the competition in batting and bowling is, in proportion, much greater than in wicket-keeping. Furthermore, a batsman or bowler, particularly the former, may lose his place in a side simply through striking a " bad patch " or run of ill-luck, to which a wicket-keeper is not subject in the same manner.

However, it is decided that the boy is going to be made into a wicket-keeper, and the next question which father has to settle, without any assistance from mother, is how he is going to start. In point of fact it very seldom occurs that anybody deliberately attempts to make a wicket-keeper of a boy. He generally drifts into it quite by chance, and subsequently never receives the tuition and attention which is devoted to the art of batting and bowling, or even fielding.

It is a pity, and the general standard of wicket-keeping which, at any rate, in amateur cricket is moderate, would be vastly improved if more boys were taken in hand when young and taught to be wicket-keepers in the same way as they are taught to be batsmen.

It should not be necessary to emphasize the importance of a wicket-keeper. An indifferent one can ruin a very strong bowling side and make their efforts a farce.

The best way to start a boy off is to take every

opportunity of bowling or throwing balls at him from any distance. Any sort of ball will do that will not bounce too high. A new tennis ball, for instance, will probably do that. Some form of " stump " ball is the best.

Always make the boy stand behind something—a single wicket or something to represent it. This is to get him accustomed to taking the ball in relation to the wicket. It will probably be best not to bother about his feet at all at this stage, but try and get him to get his hands right—fingers down, etc. (See Chapter II.) This should almost automatically get his feet right as far as moving sidways is concerned, but he may step back a bit. Now and again ask him if he can reach the stump with the ball in both hands. It is not necessary to sweep the ball towards the top of the stumps on every occasion.

It is a bad habit which may lead to snatching or, at the best, to undesirable mannerisms. Make the boy throw the ball back from where he takes it. He will soon get to learn the occasions on which the ball must be taken to the wicket with a view to stumping. That will come instinctively when he gets a batsman in front of him.

The next stage is to get him proper gloves and pads, put him in a net and bowl at him with a cricket ball. There should be no batsman, and one stump only. This stump should be just far enough from the back of the net to allow the boy freedom of movement, but close enough to prevent him from stepping back out of reach of the wicket. Bowl all sorts of length on either side of the wicket. Continue this method of practice until the position of hands and feet are satisfactory and the pupil gets the majority of balls nicely into his hands.

Simultaneously with this stage a certain amount of running out practice can be given, the ball being thrown in at one stump from varying distances. The boy may here be allowed to go through the motion of removing the bails as quick as he can, but be careful to emphasize his mistakes if he drops the ball by trying to be too quick. He will very likely do this with full pitches, which cannot be snatched at with impunity.

The next stage is to get a really good net wicket, not too fast, and allow the boy to keep behind three stumps and a batsman. The batsman should not play at anything outside his legs at all—he will have to play at a ball to keep it off his body or wicket, and he should do no more than flourish his bat at balls outside the off stump. Thus, the boy will have plenty of balls to take, and will gain experience of having his vision obstructed to *a certain extent only*.

At this period encourage him to watch the bowler's hand to see what spin is being imparted to the ball, and if there is anywhere nearby where professionals are bowling in the nets, take him and make him stand behind the net and watch their hands carefully.

It should hardly be necessary to say that all the principles laid down in Chapters II and III with regard to correct taking of the ball should be carefully observed in the two latter stages.

Now the boy is ready for match practice. The question of whether the boy, or anyone else for that matter, gains much benefit from " keeping " in a net when someone is having batting practice is rather a debatable one.

In the first place, a batsman in a net very rarely lets a ball get past him, and, if he does, it is probably a nasty one to take. Furthermore, net wickets are seldom really good. Very often the balls are old and the light indifferent, all of which makes it difficult for the wicket-keeper, and may produce a lack of confidence.

Match practice on good wickets is the thing. Once again, try and keep a boy off bad wickets.

CHAPTER XIV.

Personal Reminiscences.

Appealing.—I was keeping against Oxford University at Oxford a few years ago. J. A. Nunn had made 98 against us, when I took a ball on the leg side—one of those very close to the leg which are really taken blind—which had hit something. I paused a moment, but did not appeal, as I thought it would be bad luck for a batsman to be caught off his pad at 98. Over was then called. A. C. Wilkinson, the Army batsman, when crossing over observed the batsman grinning. Arriving at his position at short leg, he appealed to the umpire, who had just arrived alongside him. The batsman was given out. A correct decision.

Moral: Do not be too shy about appealing, and remember that you can appeal after over is called, provided another ball has not been bowled.

In Egypt, playing for H. M. Martineau's XI *v.* All Egypt, Rogers, the Gloucestershire and Army batsman, took a swing at an overpitched ball covered completely by his body. I happened to pick up the ball coming slowly over his left shoulder. I held it for a moment, looked at the bowler, and threw it back, thinking it must have hit the top of his pad. It had, as a matter of fact, hit the back of his glove. His score was then 0, but he made 50, and they won the match by one wicket.

Running Out.—The following is a curious run out incident:—

I was keeping wicket at Aldershot behind one of the best Army batsmen on a hard, fast wicket. Our bowling was none too good, and the possibilities of dismissing him seemed remote.

He chopped down and half-balled a yorker on the middle stump.

Thinking, perhaps not unnaturally, that it had gone somewhere in the region of fine leg, he took half a step forward and had a look to see if there was a possibility of a run. As a matter of fact, he had half-balled it so accurately that it merely bounced very slowly over the top of the middle stump into my hands at the moment when he took his step forward. Run out.

A Wicket-keeping Problem.—This is not a personal reminiscence, but a problem which was set to the M.C.C. Committee for solution. A batsman jumped out of his ground, the ball hit the wicket-keeper's pads, rebounded forward, hit the heel of the batsman's boot as he was unsuccessfully endeavouring to put a foot back into the crease, and came back and hit the wicket. Was the batsman stumped or run out?

The Press.—In Trinidad in 1929 I was accused of what I believe is known as " picking the bails " by the coloured editor of a daily paper.

Voce bowled the last Trinidad player, hitting the off stump pretty hard and removing, I think, both bails. The ball happened to come into my hands off the wicket, and we all walked off the ground and thought nothing more about it until an article appeared the next morning, in which the writer stated that he had seen the ball miss the wicket and " Ames' " hands strike the bails off. This was very good, as although he could see a ball missing the wicket by an inch he had failed to notice that, although Ames had been keeping in the morning, I had been keeping wicket the entire afternoon.

Incidentally, Trinidad is a particularly difficult ground on which to watch details of the play. There is always a glare, it is big, and the stands are low and badly placed. Our coloured friend always used to sit in the same place, and when the wicket-keeping incident arose he was watching the game from the angle of long leg, a particularly difficult position on any ground from which to observe a ball just outside the off stump.

In a previous article he had queried two l.b.w. decisions of that excellent umpire, Joe Hardstaff, stating that he had distinctly seen the ball pitch " one or two inches " outside the wicket. When a rival paper pointed out that he could not have been watching too carefully if he had failed to notice the change of wicket-keepers he was quite unabashed, and wrote another article maintaining that the ball had not hit the wicket, and that I had removed the bails.

Extras.—I was concerned in what, I think, must be the record number of extras. It was the end of my last term at Oxford. I attended three Commemoration Balls on successive nights, the last being the " House " Ball, which terminated at about 7 a.m. Having to take my degree at 9 a.m., I did not have an opportunity to go to bed, but, nevertheless, after the rather long ceremony, set off to Harrow to play for the O.U. Authentics against the School. Arriving at lunch time, I found that Walter Monckton, now K.C., a very good wicket-keeper, who was rather out of practice, had conceded some 20 byes out of 80 runs scored.

I took over after lunch, and what with a not unnatural fatigue, a wicket that was not too good, and some very erratic bowling, conceded a good many more byes, which brought the total to about 40 out of the score of 270. Neville Talbot, recently Bishop of Pretoria, as well as being somewhat wild in length and direction, bowled no fewer than 15 no balls which figured on the score sheet.

Added to which were a goodish percentage of leg byes, and the grand total of extras was 70.

I was always told there was a poem in the *Harrovian*, and a tree planted to celebrate this great performance by Mr. Extras, but I never saw either.

Umpires.—The worst decision I have ever seen was given by an umpire at Lima in Peru, where the M.C.C. played a match on their return from the South American tour of 1926-27.

I stumped their opening batsman when at least two yards out of his ground. He confessed to me that he heard the click of the bails before his bat had completed its follow through. However, the umpire knew his business, as the batsman increased his score from 0 to 21, and the total for the innings was 29.

We subsequently had the greatest difficulty in getting our legs out of the way of a big off-spinner bowling over, not round, the wicket.

A Skier.—It was in the previous match of the tour at Valparaiso that "Plum" Warner, following the rule that the wicket-keeper should take a skier, called to me to take one off G. O. Allen. "Plum" called the moment the ball started to go up in the air. I threaded my way through three or four slips, and started to run for all I was worth. The ball, however, had more carry on it than was at first apparent, and, going a great height, was assisted by a strong wind. Finally, it pitched very nearly a six in the deep third-man area, and I was half-way there, much to the amusement of players and spectators.

A Difficult Bowler.—I always think that "Buster" Nupen, the South African, must, on matting wickets, be one of the most difficult bowlers in the world to keep to, though Cameron takes him superbly and makes it look easy.

Bowling fast medium round the wicket, he will bring the ball back the breadth of the wicket, and it comes whistling round the batsman's body about hip high. Now and again he "runs" one several inches from the leg. He used to get great pace off the pitch, and Percy Chapman has probably rightly described him as the best bowler in the world when on matting. On grass he is not the same.

The Best Catch.—One is often asked what was the best catch one has ever seen caught at the wicket. It is quite impossible to say, but I always remember two which "Struddy" caught in one of the late Solly Joel's Ascot Sunday matches.

"Struddy" was a scorer then, and had not kept wicket that year, but he caught a low leg glide and a hard cut-down one on the off, both as good catches as anyone could wish to see. I myself that afternoon missed a very low "skier" (if that is not a contradiction of terms). I blamed the sun myself, but my fellow players attributed it to the champagne, of which there was always an abundance at Solly's luncheons.

The Camera Can Lie.—The art of cricket photography has in recent years reached a high and most interesting standard. Yet, in looking at cricket photos, it must be remembered that the camera can and does lie, and allege a wrong decision against the umpire.

A few years ago, in an Army *v.* Navy match at Lords, one of the Navy players was given out, stumped. One or two people, including Army players, doubted the correctness of the decision, and when in the evening paper a photo appeared showing the bails only just off the top of the stumps and the batsman's toe within the crease, they came to me and said, "We told you so." Subsequently, however, another photo of the same incident appeared in the Press, in which the bails were much higher in the air and the batsman's toe was only just touching the line. In the first photograph published the bails were descending, and in the later one ascending.

CHAPTER XV.

TEST MATCH WICKET-KEEPERS.

THE following is a complete list of wicket-keepers who have kept for England in Test Matches either at home or abroad, the years in which they played and the number of matches they kept in:—

Year	Match	Keeper	Matches
1876-77	v. Australia in Australia	E. Pooley	1
1878-79	v. Australia in Australia	Mr. L. Hone	1
1880	v. Australia in England	The Hon. A. Lyttleton	1
1881-82	v. Australia in Australia	R. Pilling	4
1882	v. Australia in England	The Hon. A. Lyttleton	1
1882-83	v. Australia in Australia	Mr. E. F. S. Tylecote	4
1884	v. Australia in England	Hon. A. Lyttleton	2
		R. Pilling	1
1884-85	v. Australia in Australia	J. Hunter	5
1886	v. Australia in England	Mr. E. F. S. Tylecote	2
		R. Pilling	1
1886-87	v. Australia in Australia	R. Pilling	2
1887-88	v. Australia in Australia	R. Pilling	2
1888	v. Australia in England	R. Pilling	1
		M. Sherwin	1
		H. Wood	1
1888-89	v. South Africa in S. Africa	H. Wood	2
1890	v. Australia in England	Mr. G. McGregor	2
1891-92	v. Australia in Australia	Mr. G. McGregor	3
1893	v. Australia in England	Mr. G. McGregor	3
1894-95	v. Australia in Australia	Mr. H. Philipson	4
		Mr. L. H. Gray	1
1895-96	v. South Africa in S. Africa	H. Butt	3
1896	v. Australia in England	A. Lilley	3
1897-98	v. Australia in Australia	W. Storer	5
1898-99	v. South Africa in S. Africa	W. Board	2
1899	v. Australia in England	W. Storer	1
		A. Lilley	4
1901-02	v. Australia in Australia	A. Lilley	5
1902	v. Australia in England	A. Lilley	5
1903-04	v. Australia in Australia	A. Lilley	5
1905	v. Australia in England	A. Lilley	5
1905-06	v. South Africa in S. Africa	H. Board	4
		Mr. L. J. Moon	1
1907	v. South Africa in England	A. Lilley	3
1907-08	v. Australia in Australia	J. Humphries	3
		Mr. R. A. Young	2
1909	v. Australia in England	A. Lilley	5
1909-10	v. South Africa in S. Africa	H. Strudwick	5
		Mr. N. C. Tufnell	1

			Matches.
1911-12	v. Australia in Australia	E. J. Smith	4
		H. Strudwick	1
1912	v. Australia in England	E. J. Smith	3
1912	v. South Africa in England	E. J. Smith	3
1913-14	v. South Africa in S. Africa	H. Strudwick	5
1920-21	v. Australia in Australia	H. Strudwick	4
		A. Dolphin	1
1921	v. Australia in England	G. Brown	3
		H. Strudwick	2
1922-23	v. South Africa in S. Africa	G. Brown	4
		G. Street	1
1924	v. South Africa in England	Mr. G. E. C. Wood	3
		G. Duckworth	1
		H. Strudwick	1
1924-25	v. Australia in Australia	H. Strudwick	5
1926	v. Australia in England	H. Strudwick	5
1927-28	v. South Africa in S. Africa	Capt. R. T. Stanyforth	4
		H. Elliott	1
1928	v. West Indies in England	G. Duckworth	1
		H. Elliott	1
		H. Smith	1
1928-29	v. Australia in Australia	G. Duckworth	5
1929	v. South Africa in England	G. Duckworth	4
		L. Ames	1
1929-30	v. West Indies in W. Indies	L. Ames	4
1930	v. Australia in England	G. Duckworth	5
1930-31	v. South Africa in S. Africa	G. Duckworth	3
		W. Farrimond	2
1931	v. New Zealand in England	L. Ames	3
1932	v. India in England	L. Ames	1
1932-33	v. Australia in Australia	L. Ames	5
1933	v. West Indies in England	L. Ames	3
1933-34	v. India in India	H. Elliott	2
		W. H. Levett	1
1934	v. Australia in England	L. Ames	5

Lilley, Strudwick, Duckworth and Ames stand out as the pre-eminent wicket-keepers of the past thirty-five years, or of the twentieth century.

Their test records are as follow:—

	Matches.	Stumped.	Caught.	Total.
Lilley	35	22	70	92
Strudwick	28	11	60	71
Duckworth	19	10	39	49
Ames	22	12	50	62

It is interesting to compare the batting abilities of these four.

Ames is a great deal the best, and originally secured his place in an England eleven more on account of his batting than on account of his ability behind the stumps, as he was probably not at that time the best wicket-keeper in England.

Lilley was a useful batsman—rather more than a tail-ender, and he never lost his place in an England side on account of batting, with the possible exception of one match in 1899, when Storer kept.

Strudwick and Duckworth have always been number elevens, and both have lost their places on occasions to a more likely run-getter.

In theory the best wicket-keeper available should be selected without regard to his batting ability, and this should always be adhered to in practice if one wicket-keeper is very definitely superior to his rivals.

The selectors are, however, sometimes confronted with a very awkward problem, such as the inclusion of four non-batting bowlers and a wicket-keeper which makes a very dangerous tail. The best wicket-keeper, though, is such an asset to the attack that it may often be better to weaken the bowlers on paper, as Chapman did in Australia in 1928—29, when he took the field with three regular bowlers, plus Hammond, in order to keep his batting intact, and also play Duckworth, who was then at his best.

CHAPTER XVI.

WICKET-KEEPING FEATS.

(Extracted by kind permission from " John Wisden's Cricketers' Almanack, 1934.")

12 wickets in match, ct. 8, st. 4, Pooley (E.), Surrey v. Sussex at the Oval	1868
10 wickets in match, ct. 5, st. 5, Phillips (H.), Sussex v. Surrey, at the Oval	1872
10 wickets in match, ct. 2, st. 8, Pooley (E.), Surrey v. Kent, at the Oval	1878
10 wickets in match, ct. 9, st. 1, Oates (T. W.), Nottinghamshire v. Middlesex, at Nottingham	1906
10 wickets in match, ct. 1 st. 9, Huish (F. H.), Kent v. Surrey, at the Oval	1911
10 wickets in match, ct. 9, st. 1, Hubble (J. C.), Kent v. Gloucestershire, at Cheltenham	1923
7 wickets in innings, ct. 4, st. 3, Smith (E. J.), Warwickshire v. Derbyshire, at Edgbaston	1926
7 wickets in innings, ct. 6, st. 1, Farrimond (W.), Lancashire v. Kent at Manchester	1930

Several wicket-keepers have taken as many as six in an innings.

Thirty-two wickets in 4 consecutive matches, ct. 16, st. 16, Pooley (E.) in 1868—12 (ct. 8, st. 4) v. Sussex at the Oval; 8 (ct. 4, st. 4) v. Kent at Gravesend; 6 (ct. 3, st. 3) v. Notts at the Oval, and 6 (ct. 1, st. 5) v. Lancashire at the Oval.

Three men stumped off successive balls, W. H. Brain, Gloucestershire v. Somerset, at Cheltenham, 1893.

(The bowler thus credited with the hat-trick was C. L. Townsend.)

In all Yorkshire matches Hunter (D.) caught 920 and stumped 352.

In all Sussex matches Butt (H. R.) caught 927 and stumped 274. (He also made one catch while fielding at slip.)

In all Kent matches Huish (F. H.) caught 906 and stumped 356.

In all matches for Notts, Oates (T. W.) caught 756 and stumped 233.

In first-class cricket Strudwick (H.) caught 1,235 and stumped 258. Of those wickets, 1,035 were caught and 185 stumped for Surrey.

In four consecutive innings in three matches, all for Gloucestershire in 1927, Smith (H.) allowed only one bye while 1,374 runs were being made against his side for 23 wickets. The games were: v. Yorkshire, at Gloucester; v. Surrey, at the Oval; and v. Yorkshire, at Dewsbury.

In the match at Brighton, in 1890, between Sussex and Cambridge University, Butt (H. R.), the Sussex wicket-keeper, allowed only one bye while Cambridge scored 703 for 9 wickets.

H. W. P. Middleton, playing in a House match at Repton on 10th July, 1930, for Priory v. Mitre, caught 1 and stumped 8 in an innings.

127 wickets in a season, ct. 79, st. 48, Ames (L. E. G.), of Kent ... 1929
121 wickets in a season, ct. 69, st. 52, Ames (L. E. G.), of Kent ... 1928
107 wickets in a season, ct. 77, st. 30, Duckworth (G.), of Lancashire 1928
102 wickets in a season, ct. 70, st. 32, Huish (F. H.), of Kent ... 1913
100 wickets in a season, ct. 36, st. 64, Ames (L. E. G.), of Kent ... 1932
100 wickets in a season, ct. 62, st. 38, Huish (F. H.), of Kent ... 1911
97 wickets in a season, ct. 71, st. 26, Street (G. B.), of Sussex ... 1923
97 wickets in a season, ct. 49, st. 48, Ames (L. E. G.), of Kent ... 1930
95 wickets in a season, ct. 58, st. 37, Duckworth (G.), of Lancashire 1929
91 wickets in a season, ct. 71, st. 20, Strudwick (H.), of Surrey 1903
89 wickets in a season, ct. 58, st. 31, Dolphin (A.), of Yorkshire 1919
89 wickets in a season, ct. 67, st. 22, Elliott (H.), of Derbyshire 1933
86 wickets in a season, ct. 57, st. 29, Huish (F. H.), of Kent ... 1908

www.ingramcontent.com/pod-product-compliance
Lightning Source LLC
Chambersburg PA
CBHW060214050426
42446CB00013B/3068